THE Kids' COOKBOOK

Kid-tested recipes

FROM THE WEST VILLAGE NURSERY SCHOOL

JELLYBEAN PRESS

New York • Avenel, New Jersey

A LUCAS • EVANS BOOK

Copyright © 1993 by West Village Nursery School
Illustrations copyright © 1993 by Teri Weidner
All rights reserved

First published in 1993 by JellyBean Press,
distributed by Outlet Book Company, Inc.,
a Random House Company,
40 Engelhard Avenue
Avenel, New Jersey 07001

Designer: Jean Krulis
Editorial supervision: Katherine Gleason

Manufactured in the United States

Library of Congress Cataloging-in-Publication Data
The Kids cookbook / by the West Village Nursery School : illustrated
by Teri Weidner.
p. cm.
Summary: A collection of kid-tested recipes for desserts, snacks,
lunch and supper dishes, soups, and salads.
ISBN 0-517-05589-9
1. Cookery—Juvenile literature. [1. Cookery.] I. Weidner,
Teri, ill. II. West Village Nursery School (New York, N.Y.)
TX652.5.K482 1993
641.5'123—dc20   93-16852
                                                                CIP
                                                                AC

8 7 6 5 4 3 2 1

Contents

Dynamite Desserts

Scrumptious Snacks

Cooking Glossary

A Note to Adult Helpers

This cookbook is strictly for KIDS! The recipes have been chosen by kids, cooked by kids, eaten by kids, and approved by kids. The kid-testers span almost two generations of happy young chefs attending the famous West Village Nursery School in New York City.

"Cooking with children can be many things," says one of the school's former directors. "It can be frustrating, satisfying, messy, surprising, *and* edible." She points out that for young children it is also a great learning experience. "For a three-year-old, cracking an egg can be a real adventure." For the older child, cooking is like performing magic tricks, and you get to eat the results!

Most of the recipes in this book can be easily followed by a school-aged child, with an adult's supervision. It is advised, however, that turning on and setting the oven, removing things from it, draining cooked food, and even taking hot food from the top of the stove can be dangerous for the inexperienced. The use of knives and electrical equipment should also be closely watched.

Cooking is fun. It is creative and stimulates the imagination as well as the taste buds. It is a special sharing experience.

Cooking is an important part of growing up!

Discuss the recipe you choose with an adult before you begin. Make sure you understand all the directions and which utensils and ingredients to have ready. Clean the counter you put them on.

Wear an apron to keep your clothes clean. It's good to wipe your hands on, too.

Always wash your hands first in warm, soapy water, then rinse them thoroughly. Wash the fruits and vegetables you use, too.

Potholders should always be nearby for handling hot things. It is better to have an adult do this for you. Potholders should be used to remove hot pans from the stove top or oven and to lift hot lids from pots. Have a hot pad or large potholder ready on the counter to set hot things on. Don't put a hot pan directly on a counter top. It will burn it. Turn off the flame in the oven or on the stove immediately after use. ***Never put your hands inside the oven.*** With a potholder or oven mitt, pull out the rack that the pan is sitting on a few inches before removing the pan.

Keep pot and pan handles turned inward on the stove to keep from knocking the handles and causing a spill.

Keep wiping your hands dry. Never use an electric appliance, like a blender, ***with wet hands.*** Never put or pour anything into the blender while its blades are going around.

Use a knife carefully. Never direct the blade toward yourself. Always cut on a cutting board. When the sharp side of the blade is facing down, be sure to keep your fingers out of the way. ***It is best to let an adult show you how to use a sharp knife.*** Use these rules for vegetable peelers and graters, too.

Beginning with Breakfast

FRENCH TOAST

INGREDIENTS:

4 eggs

2/3 cup milk

8 slices whole-wheat bread

2 tablespoons butter or
    margarine for frying

HAVE READY:

Shallow bowl

Fork

Measuring cup

Large plate

Frying pan

Spatula

1. Break the eggs into the bowl. Beat with the fork until all yellow.

2. Add the milk and stir well.

3. Dip the bread slices one by one in the egg mixture. Coat both sides. Put the bread on the plate.

4. In the frying pan, melt the butter over low heat.

5. Cook one egg-coated slice until it is brown. Turn with the spatula and brown the other side.

6. Cook the slices, one at a time. If the frying pan gets dry, add more butter.

7. Serve the French toast with syrup or jam.

For a different flavor, add ¼ teaspoon cinnamon to the egg mixture. Or add ½ teaspoon vanilla extract.

Use slices of day-old Italian bread or challah (a rich egg bread) instead of whole-wheat bread for a nice variation.

INGREDIENTS:

1½ cups flour

2½ teaspoons baking powder

3 tablespoons sugar

¾ teaspoon salt

3 tablespoons butter

2 eggs

1¼ cup milk

2 extra tablespoons butter for frying

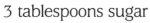

HAVE READY:

Large mixing bowl

Measuring cups

Measuring spoons

Large mixing spoon

Small pan for melting butter

Small bowl

Fork

Large frying pan

Soup spoon

Spatula

1. In the large bowl, mix together the flour, baking powder, sugar, and salt.

2. In the small pan, melt the 3 tablespoons of butter over low heat. Set aside.

3. Break the eggs into the small bowl. Beat them with a fork until all yellow.

4. To make the batter, stir the eggs into the flour mixture. Slowly pour in the milk, stirring constantly. Then mix in the melted butter.

5. Heat 1 extra tablespoon of butter in the large frying pan.

6. For each pancake, pour 1 soup spoon of batter into the pan. You can cook two or three pancakes at once, adding extra butter when necessary.

7. Cook the pancakes over medium heat until they are bubbly on top. Then turn the pancakes over with the spatula and cook the other side until light brown.

8. Serve the pancakes with butter and syrup.

You can make **Fruity Pancakes** by adding 1 cup grated or chopped apples, pears, peaches, or fresh berries to the batter before cooking.

PERFECT POPOVERS

INGREDIENTS:

Small pat of butter or margarine
    to grease muffin tin

2 eggs

1 cup milk

1 cup flour

¼ teaspoon salt

HAVE READY:

Muffin tin

Mixing bowl

Whisk

Measuring cups

Measuring spoons

Mixing spoon

Potholders

1. Preheat the oven to 475°.

2. Grease the muffin tin and put it in the oven to heat.

3. Break the eggs into the bowl, then whisk them until frothy.

4. Pour in the milk.

5. Add the flour and salt to make the batter.

6. Beat hard with the whisk for 2 minutes.

7. Using potholders, take the hot muffin tin out of the oven.

8. Pour the batter into the muffin tin. Fill each cup about one-third full.

9. Bake at 475° for 15 minutes. Reduce the heat to 350° and bake for 30 minutes more until popovers are brown and puffy.

10. Using potholders, remove the tin from the oven. Use a fork to remove the popovers from the pan. Serve them hot with butter and jam.

FRESH SWEET BUTTER

INGREDIENTS:

½ pint heavy cream

HAVE READY:

1 pint jar with tight-fitting lid

1. Pour the cream into the jar.

2. Screw the lid on the jar. Be sure it's tight.

3. Shake the cream until it makes a lump of butter.

4. Spread the fresh butter on the popovers.

There will be some liquid left in the jar. That's buttermilk! Drink it or use it in cooking.

Yummy Lunches
and Dinners

CHILI CON CARNE

INGREDIENTS:

1 medium onion

1 tablespoon vegetable oil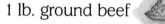

1 lb. ground beef

1 28-oz. can tomato puree

1 cup water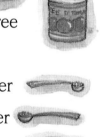

¼ teaspoon garlic powder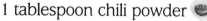

1 tablespoon chili powder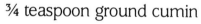

¾ teaspoon ground cumin

1 can kidney beans, drained

HAVE READY:

Small knife

Cutting board

Large, heavy pot with lid

Measuring spoons

Wooden spoon

Measuring cup

Can opener

Potholders

1. Peel the onion, then chop it coarsely.

2. Heat the oil in the pot. Add the onion and cook it until it's soft. Stir it often. Add the beef and cook it over medium heat until it is brown. Stir it while it is cooking. Have an adult drain off the fat.

3. Stir in the tomato puree, water, garlic powder, chili powder, and cumin.

4. Cover the pot. Make the heat very low and simmer for 1½ hours, stirring occasionally.

5. Stir in the beans. Simmer for 10 minutes more.

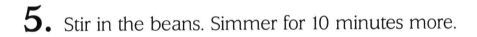

6. Let the chili cool a little, then serve in bowls with corn bread or crackers.

Instead of beef, you can use ground turkey or extra beans and vegetables. It's the spices that count in chili!

If you like, you can sprinkle grated cheese on top and serve chopped raw onion on the side.

MACARONI AND CHEESE

INGREDIENTS:

½ lb. cheddar cheese
    (to make 1 cup grated)

4 cups water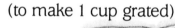

1 cup uncooked macaroni

1 tablespoon butter

2 tablespoons flour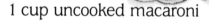

¼ teaspoon salt

Pinch of pepper

1 cup milk

HAVE READY:

Grater

Large pot

Measuring cup

Measuring spoons

Saucepan

Wooden spoon

Colander

9- x 13-inch baking pan

Potholders

1. Grate the cheese.

2. In a large pot, bring the water to a boil.

3. Stir in the macaroni. Check the package for how long the macaroni should cook and follow directions. Do not overcook.

4. In the saucepan, melt the butter over very low heat.

5. Add the flour, salt, and pepper. Stir and cook until the mixture is bubbly.

6. Remove the pan from the heat. Slowly stir in the milk to make the sauce.

7. Put the pan back on low heat. Cook until the sauce boils, stirring constantly.

8. Have an adult drain the cooked macaroni in the colander.

9. Preheat the oven to 375°.

10. In the baking pan, mix together the grated cheese and the macaroni. Cover with the sauce.

11. Bake for 30 minutes or until the top is brown and the sauce is bubbly.

FIESTA RICE

INGREDIENTS:

1 green pepper

2 celery stalks

1 small onion

4 tablespoons margarine

1 cup white rice

2 cups chicken broth

1 teaspoon salt

¼ teaspoon pepper

¼ teaspoon saffron threads

1 tablespoon hot water

1 16-oz. can tomatoes

HAVE READY:

Small knife

Cutting board

Large, heavy pot

Wooden spoon

Measuring cups

Measuring spoons

A cup

Potholders

Fiesta Rice tastes great with Baked "Fried" Chicken Legs.

1. Wash the pepper and celery. Cut away the pepper's stem and the white pith inside. Discard the seeds. Peel the onion. Cut the vegetables into bite-sized cubes.

2. In the pot, melt the margarine over low heat. Add the vegetables. Cook for 5 minutes, stirring constantly.

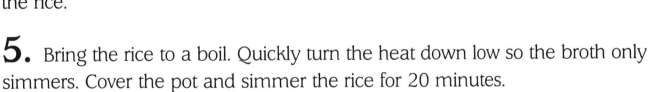

3. Add the rice, chicken broth, salt, and pepper. Stir well.

4. In a cup, mix the saffron with the hot water. When the water turns very orangey-red, add it to the rice.

5. Bring the rice to a boil. Quickly turn the heat down low so the broth only simmers. Cover the pot and simmer the rice for 20 minutes.

6. Add the tomatoes and cook about 5 minutes more or until the rice absorbs all the broth.

BAKED "FRIED" CHICKEN LEGS

INGREDIENTS:

3 cups cornflakes

10 chicken legs

¾ stick butter

Salt

Pepper

Paprika

HAVE READY:

Measuring cup

Plastic bag (self seal is best)

Rolling pin

Mixing bowl

Paper towels

Small frying pan

Tongs or fork

9- x 13-inch baking pan

Potholders

1. Preheat the oven to 400°.

2. Put the cornflakes in the plastic bag. Put the bag on the counter and crush the cornflakes with the rolling pin. Put the crushed cornflakes in the mixing bowl.

3. Wash the chicken legs, then pat them dry with paper towels.

4. In the frying pan, melt the butter over low heat. Remove the pan from the heat. Using a fork or tongs, dip a chicken leg in the melted butter.

5. Then, roll the chicken in the cornflakes.

6. Put it in the baking pan. Repeat with each chicken leg. Then sprinkle them with salt, pepper, and paprika.

7. Bake for 55 minutes or until the chicken is golden brown. Use potholders to remove the pan from the oven.

After you wash the chicken, you can remove the skin if you want to cut down on fat.

THE CHEESIEST LASAGNA EVER

INGREDIENTS:

1 lb. ground beef

½ teaspoon dried oregano

Pepper to taste

1 15-oz. jar spaghetti sauce

12 cups water

1 lb. lasagna noodles

8 oz. mozzarella cheese

1 pint ricotta cheese

⅓ cup grated Parmesan cheese

HAVE READY:

Large frying pan

Wooden spoon

Measuring spoons

Very large pot

Measuring cups

Colander

Grater or knife

Large baking dish

Potholders

1. In the frying pan, cook the ground beef, stirring constantly, until it is brown. Add the oregano and a little pepper. Have an adult drain off the fat.

2. Add the spaghetti sauce and cook for 5 minutes. Remove the pan from the heat and set aside.

3. In a large pot, bring the water to a boil. Add the lasagna noodles. Check the package for how long they should cook and follow directions.

4. Have an adult drain the noodles. Put them back in the pot with cold water so they don't stick together.

5. Preheat the oven to 350°.

6. Grate or thinly slice the mozzarella cheese.

7. In the baking dish, make a layer of noodles. Cover with the meat sauce, then make a layer of mozzarella and a layer of ricotta. Repeat three times, ending with a layer of Parmesan cheese.

Turn the page for step 8.

8. Bake for 30 minutes.

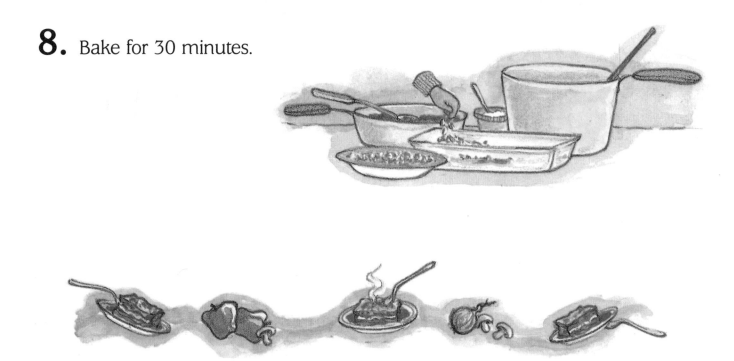

The Cheesiest Lasagna Ever
Instead of the ground beef, substitute the following vegetables:

1 small onion (chopped)
2 green peppers (chopped)
½ pound fresh mushrooms (sliced)

In the frying pan, cook the onion in 2 tablespoons olive oil.

Add the green peppers and the mushrooms.

When the vegetables are soft, add the oregano, pepper, and the spaghetti sauce.

Follow the lasagna recipe, starting with step 3.

Super Soups
and Salads,
Breads and Muffins

muffins 75¢
apricot bars $1.00
carrot Soup $1.00
+ lots more...

STONE SOUP

INGREDIENTS:

2 carrots, scraped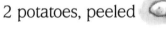

2 celery stalks, washed

2 potatoes, peeled

1 medium onion, peeled

1 large, clean stone!

1 28-oz. can tomatoes

3 cups chicken broth

1 teaspoon salt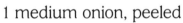

1 bay leaf

¼ teaspoon pepper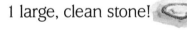

½ cup alphabet pasta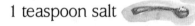

HAVE READY:

Small knife

Cutting board

Large, heavy pot with lid

Measuring cup

Measuring spoons

Ladle

Potholders

1. Cut the carrots, celery, potatoes, and onion into bite-sized pieces. Put them into the pot.

2. Add the stone, tomatoes, chicken broth, salt, bay leaf, and pepper. Mix well.

3. Cook on medium-high heat. When the soup starts to boil, turn heat down to low and cover the pot. Simmer for 30 minutes.

4. Add the pasta and cook for 10 minutes more.

5. Let the soup cool a bit. Ladle it into bowls, removing the bay leaf, and serve.

This famous soup comes from a folktale. A hungry traveler convinces a stingy peasant that he can make a delicious soup just by boiling water with a "magic" stone. "But of course it would taste better if you added a pinch of salt, or an onion, or perhaps a carrot or two and, of course, a potato…" and on and on.

Naturally, the soup was delicious, and the foolish peasant thought it was all because of the "magic" stone. Perhaps you can fool your friends, too!

CARROT SOUP

INGREDIENTS:

8 carrots, scraped

5 medium potatoes, peeled

1 medium onion, peeled

2 tablespoons butter

6 cups chicken broth

½ teaspoon thyme

1 bay leaf

2 cups milk

½ teaspoon sugar

½ teaspoon Worcestershire sauce

salt and pepper to taste

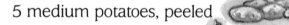

HAVE READY:

Small knife

Cutting board

Large, heavy pot with lid

Measuring cups

Measuring spoons

Slotted spoon

Blender

Mixing spoon

Ladle

Potholders

1. Slice the carrots. Cut the potatoes into cubes. Coarsely chop the onion.

2. In the pot, melt the butter. Add the onion and cook over medium heat for 10 minutes. Stir occasionally.

3. Add the carrots, potatoes, chicken broth, thyme, and bay leaf. Stir well.

4. Cover the pan and cook over low heat for 20 minutes or until the vegetables are soft.

5. Turn off the heat. Let the vegetables cool. Using a slotted spoon, transfer the vegetables from the pot to the blender. Keep the liquid. Throw away the bay leaf.

6. Puree the vegetables in the blender. You might need to add some liquid from the pot. Have an adult help you.

7. Put the pureed vegetables back into the pot with the liquid. Mix well.

8. Stir in the milk, sugar, Worcestershire sauce, salt, and pepper.

9. Mix well and cook over low heat until the soup just begins to boil. Ladle into bowls and serve.

Carrot soup is not just good *hot* on a *cold* day. It's also good *cold* on a *hot* day.

FANTASTIC FRUIT SALAD

INGREDIENTS:

1 apple, washed

2 bananas, peeled

2 oranges, peeled

1 cup grapes, washed

½ cup sour cream

1 tablespoon honey

1 tablespoon orange juice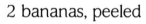

HAVE READY:

Small knife

Cutting board

Big bowl

Small bowl

Measuring cups

Measuring spoons

Mixing spoon

1. Peel and core the apple and cut it into bite-sized pieces.

2. Slice the bananas.

3. Divide the oranges into segments.

4. Arrange the banana slices on the bottom of a big bowl. Put the remaining fruit on top.

5. Chill in the refrigerator for 1 hour.

6. To make the dressing, in a small bowl mix together the sour cream, honey, and orange juice.

7. When you are ready to serve the salad, pour the dressing over the fruit and mix gently.

8. Serve in small bowls.

"HALLOWEEN" SALAD

INGREDIENTS:

10 carrots

2 cups raisins

HAVE READY:

Vegetable peeler

Grater

Bowl

Small bowl

Measuring cup

Mixing spoon

FOR DRESSING (optional):

½ cup olive oil

3 tablespoons lemon juice

Salt and pepper to taste

1. Peel and wash the carrots, then grate them into a bowl.

2. Stir in the raisins.

3. To make the dressing, in a small bowl mix together the olive oil, lemon juice, salt, and pepper. Mix well. Then pour over the salad and mix well.

4. Chill the salad in the refrigerator before serving.

CORNY CORN BREAD

INGREDIENTS:

Small pat of butter or
   margarine to grease pan

1 cup cornmeal

1 cup white flour

3 tablespoons sugar

3 teaspoons baking powder

½ teaspoon salt

1 cup milk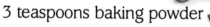

1 egg

¼ cup vegetable oil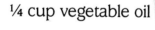

HAVE READY:

8- x 8-inch baking pan

2 mixing bowls

Measuring spoons

Measuring cup

Mixing spoon

Potholders

Wire rack

Knife

1. Preheat the oven to 450°.

2. Grease the pan with butter or margarine.

3. In one bowl, mix together the cornmeal, flour, sugar, baking powder, and salt.

4. In the other bowl, mix together the milk, egg, and oil.

5. Stir the egg mixture into the flour mixture to make a batter. Mix well.

6. Pour the batter into the greased baking pan.

7. Bake for 20 to 25 minutes or until edges of the corn bread start to brown. Using potholders, carefully remove the pan from the oven.

8. Put the pan on a wire rack. When the corn bread is cool, cut it into 2-inch squares and serve.

This bread is great with chili or soup.

APPLE MUFFINS

INGREDIENTS:

Small pat of butter or
　　margarine to grease muffin tin

2 large apples

1 cup white flour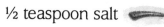

1 cup whole-wheat pastry flour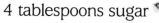

4 teaspoons baking powder

½ teaspoon salt

4 tablespoons sugar

½ teaspoon cinnamon

1 egg

1 cup milk

½ stick butter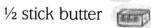

HAVE READY:

12-cup muffin tin

Small knife

Cutting board

3 mixing bowls

Measuring cups

Measuring spoons

Mixing spoon

Eggbeater or fork

Small pan

Potholders

Wire rack

1. Preheat the oven to 350°.

2. Grease the muffin tin.

3. Peel and chop the apples.

4. In a bowl, mix together the flour, baking powder, salt, 2 tablespoons of sugar, and the cinnamon.

5. In another mixing bowl, beat the egg with the milk.

6. In the small pan, melt the butter over low heat.

7. In the third bowl, mix the apples with the melted butter and the remaining 2 tablespoons of sugar.

8. Add the milk mixture to the flour mixture to make a batter. Mix well.

9. Stir in the apples.

Turn the page for steps 10, 11, and 12.

10. Spoon the batter into the muffin tin. Fill each cup two-thirds full.

11. Bake for 35 minutes.

12. Let the muffins cool for 5 minutes. Then with the potholders, turn them out of the tin and put them on a wire rack to cool.

For **Orange Muffins**, use 1 cup of orange juice instead of milk. Grate the peel of 1 orange using the small teeth of the grater and add to the batter instead of the apples.

For **Blueberry Muffins**, don't use cinnamon. Use 1 cup fresh or frozen blueberries instead of apples.

Dynamite
Desserts

THUMBPRINT BUTTER COOKIES

INGREDIENTS:

2 sticks of butter
     at room temperature

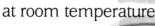

4 tablespoons sugar

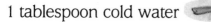

1 tablespoon cold water

1 teaspoon vanilla extract

2 cups flour

Apricot or raspberry jam

1 cup powdered sugar

HAVE READY:

Mixing bowl

Measuring cups

Mixing spoon

Measuring spoons

2 cookie sheets

Potholders

Spatula

Wire rack

Shallow bowl

1. Preheat the oven to 350°.

2. In the mixing bowl, mix the butter and sugar together.

3. Add the water and vanilla extract. Mix well.

4. Add the flour a half cup at a time. Mix to make the dough.

5. Divide the dough into 30 pieces. Roll each piece into a ball.

6. Arrange the balls one-half inch apart on the cookie sheet. Put 15 balls on each sheet.

7. Press your thumb into the center of each ball.

8. Fill the thumb hole with a spoonful of apricot or raspberry jam.

9. Bake for 15 to 20 minutes. If the edges of the cookies are brown, they are done. If not, bake a little longer.

10. With the potholders, remove the cookie sheet from the oven. Allow to cool a few minutes. Using a spatula, transfer the cookies from the sheet to the wire rack to continue cooling.

11. Put the powdered sugar into the shallow bowl. Roll the cookies in it.

APRICOT BARS

INGREDIENTS:

1½ cups flour

1 teaspoons baking powder

1 cup brown sugar

1½ cups oatmeal

1½ sticks butter

1 cup apricot jam

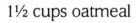
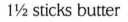

HAVE READY:

Mixing bowl

Mixing spoon

Measuring cups

Measuring spoons

9- x 13-inch baking pan

Potholders

1. Preheat the oven to 350°.

2. In a mixing bowl, mix the flour, baking powder, brown sugar, and oatmeal together.

3. Cut in the butter and mix until crumbly.

4. Pat two-thirds of the mixture into the baking pan.

5. Spread the jam on top.

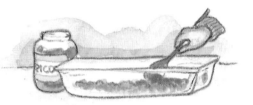

6. Cover with the remaining oatmeal mixture.

7. Bake at 350° for 30 minutes.

8. Allow to cool in the pan. Then cut into bars.

CUSTARD RICE PUDDING

INGREDIENTS:

3 eggs

½ cup cooked rice

½ cup sugar

¼ teaspoon salt

3½ cups milk

1 teaspoon vanilla extract

Ground nutmeg

HAVE READY:

Mixing bowl

Eggbeater

Measuring spoons

Measuring cups

Mixing spoon

9- x 13-inch baking dish

Large baking dish

Potholders

1. Preheat the oven to 300°.

2. Break the eggs into the bowl. Beat them until frothy.

3. Add the rice, sugar, salt, milk, and vanilla extract. Mix well.

4. Pour the rice mixture into the shallow baking dish.

5. Sprinkle with nutmeg.

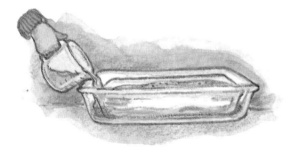

6. Put the shallow baking dish into the large baking dish. Pour a cup or two of cold water into the large baking dish.

7. Bake for 1½ hours.

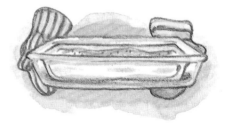

8. With potholders, take the baking dishes from the oven. Serve the pudding warm or cool.

LICK-YOUR-FINGERS CHOCOLATE

INGREDIENTS:

Small pat of butter or margarine
    to grease cookie sheets

2¼ cups flour

1 teaspoon baking soda

1 teaspoon salt

2 sticks butter at room temperature

¾ cup sugar

¾ cup brown sugar

1 teaspoon vanilla extract

⅓ cup water

2 eggs

1 12-oz. package semisweet chocolate chips

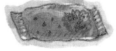

HAVE READY:

2 cookie sheets

2 large mixing bowls

Measuring cups

Measuring spoons

Flour sifter

Mixing spoon

Potholders

Spatula

Wire rack

1. Preheat the oven to 375°.

CHIP COOKIES

2. Grease the cookie sheets.

3. Sift the flour, baking soda, and salt together into one mixing bowl.

4. In the other mixing bowl, mix the butter and sugars together. Add the vanilla extract, water, and eggs and mix well.

5. Add the flour mixture to the other mixture. Stir well to form the dough.

6. Stir in the chocolate chips.

7. Drop the dough by teaspoonfuls onto the greased cookie sheets. The teaspoonfuls should be 1 inch apart. Bake in 2 or 3 batches.

8. Bake for 10 minutes or until the cookies are brown on the edges.

Turn the page for step 9.

9. With potholders, remove the cookie sheet from the oven. Use a spatula to transfer the cookies from the cookie sheet to a wire rack to cool.

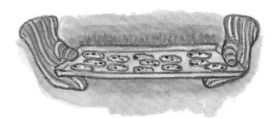

As a variation, add 1 cup chopped nuts or one cup raisins to the dough when you add the chocolate chips.

Scrumptious Snacks

ALPHABET PRETZELS

INGREDIENTS:

Small pat of butter or margarine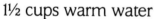
   to grease cookie sheet

1 package dry yeast

1½ cups warm water

1 tablespoon sugar

1 teaspoon salt

4 cups flour

1 egg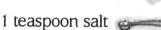

Coarse salt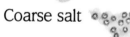

HAVE READY:

2 cookie sheets

Mixing bowl

Measuring cups

Measuring spoons

Mixing spoon

Clean surface for kneading

Small bowl

Fork

Pastry brush

Potholders

Spatula

Wire rack

1. Preheat the oven to 425°.

2. Grease the cookie sheets.

54

3. In the mixing bowl, dissolve the yeast in the water.

4. Add the sugar, salt, and flour. Mix well to make dough.

5. Turn the dough out onto a clean, floured surface. Knead the dough until it is smooth.

6. Divide the dough into 10 pieces. Roll each piece into a strip. Shape each strip into a letter. Put 5 pretzels on each cookie sheet.

7. Break the egg into the small bowl. With the fork beat the egg until it is frothy.

8. Brush the pretzels with the beaten egg and sprinkle with a little coarse salt.

9. Bake for 12 minutes.

10. Remove the pretzels with the spatula and let them cool on the wire rack.

You can make twists or other shapes. Or try making 20 small pretzels. These will bake in only 8 minutes.

OPEN SESAME CRACKERS

INGREDIENTS:

1¾ cups whole-wheat flour

¼ cup sesame seeds

¾ teaspoon salt

⅓ cup olive oil

½ cup water

HAVE READY:

Large mixing bowl

Measuring cups

Measuring spoons

Mixing spoon

Cookie sheet

Spatula

Plate

Potholder

1. Preheat the oven to 350°.

2. In the large bowl, mix together the flour, sesame seeds, and salt. Add the oil and mix well.

3. Add a little water. Stir. Keep adding water a little at a time and stirring until a dough is formed.

4. Roll the dough into 12 small balls. On a clean, floured surface, flatten the balls.

5. Arrange the crackers on the cookie sheet.

6. Bake for 20 minutes or until the crackers are brown around the edges. Using potholders, remove the cookie sheet from the oven.

7. With the spatula, transfer the crackers to a plate. Serve when cool.

Cooking Glossary

Beat To stir hard with a whisk or fork. Tilt the bowl toward you just a little. Also called "whipping."

Boil To cook on high heat until big bubbles roll.

Break an egg To crack the egg on the rim of a bowl. Insert both thumbnails in the crack and pull the shell apart slowly over the bowl.

Chop To cut into small pieces with a knife. To make really tiny pieces is called "mincing."

Drain To pour contents into a colander placed in the sink to get rid of the liquid.

Grate To make tiny pieces by rubbing the fruit or vegetable against a grater. A bowl beneath catches the pieces.

Grease To rub a little oil, butter, or margarine on the surfaces of a pan or baking dish to keep food from sticking.

Knead To squeeze and push dough back and forth on a clean, floured surface; then turn it over and repeat until the dough is smooth and springy.

Mash To crush again and again, like mashed potatoes. Usually done with a masher.

Mix To stir ingredients together slowly until they are well blended.

Peel To cut away the skin of a fruit or vegetable; best done with a peeler.

Preheat To turn on the oven to warm up to the right cooking temperature before putting the food inside to cook.

Puree To make almost a liquid, usually in a blender.

Roll To roll on a clean, floured surface, with a rolling pin or your hands, into the shape you want.

Sift To pass (dry ingredients, usually flour) through a sieve or sifter.

Simmer To cook on a stove over very low heat so that the liquid bubbles only a little bit.

Slice To cut a thin, flat piece.

Stir To move a mixing spoon in a circular motion to blend ingredients or to keep them from sticking to the cooking pot.

FOOD FAIR TODAY!!

Super • • • •
Soups + Salads
Breads + Muffins

Scrumptious
Snacks

dynamite
Desserts